Hey Teacher...
Real Talk!

Hey Teacher...
Real Talk!

Ina Perkins

iUniverse LLC
Bloomington

Hey Teacher . . . Real Talk!

iUniverse books may be ordered through booksellers or by contacting:

iUniverse LLC
1663 Liberty Drive
Bloomington, IN 47403
www.iuniverse.com
1-800-Authors (1-800-288-4677)

ISBN: 978-1-4759-9807-8 (sc)
ISBN: 978-1-4759-9808-5 (ebk)

Printed in the United States of America

iUniverse rev. date: 07/22/2013

A GIFT FOR:

_____

FROM:

_____

Hey Teacher . . . Real Talk

 Introduction

This is a practical common sense book for teachers. The advice written in a child-like perspective is practical and could be adapted for anyone in the profession of teaching. This is from the mind of a parent who was once a child, a student, a teacher, a supervisor of teachers and who continues to be an advocate for children. Read it, meditate on it, speak it, learn from it and apply it and you will be surprised how the practical common sense sayings in this book can make such a powerful impact in your life, in your classroom and in the lives of the children you touch. If you want to prosper in your career you must not only apply your book knowledge but also the practical common sense knowledge and that's **real talk**!

 # Dedication

I dedicate this book to my mother, Betty Chambers, for being the greatest mother in the world and for teaching me the small, but important things of life.

To my children DeOndre and LaBetra I thank you for sharing and allowing your mother to sow positive seeds into the lives of many other children.

To my husband, Eddie, who always encourages me and helps me to see pass what I see and to be all that God has predestine me to be.

To my sisters Sharman and Vanessa thank you for believing in my dreams.

To my good friend Dr. Charletta Sudduth for your input into my dreams.

To my church family thank you for helping me to believe in myself and the love of God.

To my family, friends and love ones thank you for your love and your prayers.

To all the people that are sowing good seeds into the lives of children may God bless you!

SEEDS

 # Hey Teacher . . .

There are great treasures on the inside of me and God has given you the key to help unlock some of those treasures.

 Hey Teacher . . .

When you invest in me you are investing in the future.
You are investing in the neighborhood.
You are investing in the community.
You are investing in the state.
You are investing in the nation.
You are investing in the world.

 # Hey Teacher . . .

My life is a garden planted with an assortment of seeds. The seeds that are planted in my life have the ability to produce much fruit and they shall come to harvest one day. I beg you please plant good seeds in my garden.

 # Hey Teacher . . .

I am so sorry for the not so good seeds that have been planted in your life that have now come to harvest. Please don't take it out on me! Please don't make me pay the price for them!

 Hey Teacher . . .

Please be patient with me. God is not through with me yet and please be patient with yourself because God is not through with you either!

# Hey Teacher . . .

Please speak words of life and not death to me or about me. Your words carry power!

 Hey Teacher . . .

Please don't silence my voice!

 Hey Teacher . . .

Your actions speak louder than your words.

 # Hey Teacher . . .

Your worth is priceless! You can never get paid for your worth. The seed that you sow into the lives of children can never ever have a monetary value placed on them!

 # Hey Teacher . . .

One day you will reap the harvest from the seeds you have planted in the lives of children.

 # Hey Teacher . . .

I am unique
and every child that you teach is unique.

 # Hey Teacher . . .

I can succeed.
Yes I Can!

Hey Teacher . . .

Love covers a multitude of faults so please show me love.

EXPECTATIONS

 Hey Teacher . . .

Thank you for not allowing your expectations for me to be based on behaviors, situations, circumstances and outward appearances.

 # Hey Teacher . . .

Thank you for not allowing your expectations for me to be based on prestige, power and money.

 Hey Teacher . . .

Thank you for not allowing your expectations for me to be based on what you see or how you feel about me.

 # Hey Teacher . . .

Thank you for basing your expectations for me on love, dreams, desires and deep inward possibilities.

 Hey Teacher . . .

I am not perfect.
I will make mistakes please help me to learn from my mistakes, don't hold them against me.

# Hey Teacher . . .

Please know that you make mistakes too just learn from them and keep on moving!

Hey Teacher . . .

Know that my small world may look different from your big world and please don't impart your big world on me, but allow me the time to explore, learn, enjoy and live my small world. I only live in this small world for a short time. Don't force me out!

 # Hey Teacher . . .

When I share secrets from my little world with you please don't blow it off like you don't care at least not in front of me. It just might be the secret that will save my mom's life; it just might be the secret that will keep me safe.

PARNTERSHIP
PARENTS

 # Hey Teacher . . .

Please don't hold me accountable for my parent's mistakes!

 # Hey Teacher . . .

I love my parents so please don't talk bad about them.

 Hey Teacher . . .

Take time to get to know my parents and you will see there are treasures on the inside of them also.

 # Hey Teacher . . .

Don't forget I am a product of my parents so the way you feel about them you may also feel the same way about me knowingly or unknowingly.

 Hey Teacher . . .

Part of my school success depends on the partnership that you and my parents build.

 Hey Teacher . . .

This partnership should be like a blank canvas with me as the common goal. You and my parents each have a paintbrush working together to paint a beautiful picture **(my school success).**

BEHAVIOR

PROBLEMS

Hey Teacher . . .

My past does not determine my future, if I had a bad day yesterday please don't punish me for it today! If I have an off day today don't hold it against me tomorrow!

 # Hey Teacher . . .

If I am having behavior problems don't only blame me and my home but please take the time to check the classroom environment.

Hey Teacher . . .

Could it be that it's the middle of the school year and you still have the same manipulatives out?

 Hey Teacher . . .

Could it be that the dramatic play area is still set up as housekeeping with the same stuff nothing taken out, nothing added?

 Hey Teacher . . .

Could it be you, that's having an off day?

 # Hey Teacher . . .

Could it be too many environmental distractions for me?

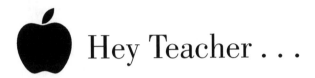

Hey Teacher . . .

Could it be that the classroom is cluttered and junky?

Hey Teacher . . .

Could it be too many things hanging on the walls and hanging from the ceiling?

 Hey Teacher . . .

Could it be the environment is not set-up for me to learn?

 Hey Teacher . . .

Many outside influences that I have no control over may be attributing to my behavior problems.

 Hey Teacher . . .

My behavior problems may be attributed to the fact that my family and I had to stay in the shelter last night.

 Hey Teacher . . .

My behavior problems may be attributed to the fact that my mom and dad argue and fight all the time and I tell them to stop but they don't listen to me and they just keep on fighting.

 Hey Teacher . . .

My behavior problems may be attributed to the fact that I haven't eaten since yesterday.

 # Hey Teacher . . .

My behavior problems may be attributed to the fact that there are fifteen people living in our two bedroom apartment.

 Hey Teacher . . .

My behavior problems may be attributed to the fact that my body chemicals are off balance and doing their own thing and it is making it very difficult for me to keep my body still and to listen.

 Hey Teacher . . .

My behavior problems may be attributed to the fact that my mom bit my arm and left her teeth marks, remember I showed you!

 Hey Teacher . . .

My behavior problems may be attributed to the fact that I didn't get enough sleep last night.

 # Hey Teacher . . .

My behavior problems may be attributed to the fact that I just might be experiencing things in my life that no child should be experiencing!

CLASSROOM
ENVIRONMENT

 Hey Teacher . . .

Delegate
Don't Wait!

 # Hey Teacher . . .

When I am having a challenging day please don't take it personal I am just trying to figure out my little upside down world.

 Hey Teacher . . .

Yes, your outside life does affect the classroom.

 Hey Teacher . . .

Just want you to know when you and your coworkers don't get along and work together it disrupts the classroom environment.

 # Hey Teacher . . .

— Please work together
— Work out disagreements
— Encourage and support one another
— Carry your work load
— Speak words of life to each other and about each other!

Hey Teacher . . .

Please don't holler across the room at me because I get enough of that outside of school. Please come over to me and talk to me at my level. This will help me to understand what I am doing wrong and it will also give you a chance to help me learn to problem solve to make better decisions.

 Hey Teacher . . .

Thank you for making the learning environment secure for me to be a risk-taker and feel good about learning from my mistakes.

 Hey Teacher . . .

Thank you for structure and routine which helps to teach me consistency, Predictability, dependability, social skills, self-help skills, trust and so much more.

 Hey Teacher . . .

Thank you for making me feel safe here at school . . . sometimes my life outside school can be so very scary!

 # Hey Teacher . . .

Today may be my last day in your classroom, so please do the best job that you can do today!

PLAY

LARGE

MOTOR

Hey Teacher . . .

Large motor time is really important to my little body. Please don't take it away from me because I had a hard time sitting at story time or listening throughout the day. If I can't participate in all of it please allow me to participate in part of it.

 # Hey Teacher . . .

If your body doesn't feel like participating in large motor time please, please don't stop mine!

 Hey Teacher . . .

Did you know that you can learn a lot about me by watching me at play?

 Hey Teacher . . .

When you watch me at play you can learn who my friends are.

 # Hey Teacher . . .

When you watch me at play you can learn how developed or undeveloped my large motor skills are.

 Hey Teacher . . .

When you watch me at play you can learn if I am a leader or follower.

 # Hey Teacher . . .

When you watch me at play you can learn the stages of social development I am experiencing.

 # Hey Teacher . . .

When you watch me at play you can learn what my interests are and you can use that to guide my learning in other areas.

 Hey Teacher . . .

When you watch me at play believe it or not you can also learn about my home life.

 # Hey Teacher . . .

When you watch me at play you can learn about my language development.

 Hey Teacher . . .

When you watch me at play you can learn about my ability to comprehend.

COMMUNITY

CULTURE

 # Hey Teacher . . .

Please learn about my culture it will open your eyes to misconceptions that you may have about my behavior, my family and me.

 Hey Teacher . . .

Please learn about my community where I live and where you work.

ASSUMPTIONS

 Hey Teacher . . .

Please don't always assume that I know how to do the small things.

 # Hey Teacher . . .

Please don't assume that I know how to line up and walk in a straight line.

 Hey Teacher . . .

Please don't assume that I know how to follow a schedule.

 Hey Teacher . . .

Please don't assume that I know how to sit down to eat and stay there until I am done.

 Hey Teacher . . .

Please don't assume that I know how to snap my pants.

 Hey Teacher . . .

Please don't assume that I know how to tie my shoes.

 Hey Teacher . . .

Please don't assume that I know how to take off my coat and hang it up.

 Hey Teacher . . .

Please don't assume that I know how to play with others.

 Hey Teacher . . .

Please don't assume that I know how to follow more than a one-step direction.

 Hey Teacher . . .

Please don't assume that I know how to raise my hand.

 Hey Teacher . . .

The assumption list can go on and on!

 # Hey Teacher . . .

It's not my fault
That I miss many days of school
That I am late for school
That I am sick
That I am hungry
That I smell funny
That my hair is not combed
It's just not my fault!

 Hey Teacher . . .

It's not my fault
That my clothes are dirty and to little
That I don't learn the way you think I
should learn
That I don't act the way you think I should
act
That I look the way I do
That I am in your class
It's just not my fault!

CREATIVITY

 Hey Teacher . . .

You are a creative being by nature, please seek and use your creativity to help me learn.

 Hey Teacher . . .

Think outside the box!
Don't limit yourself!

 Hey Teacher . . .

Dare to be different!
Dare to be you!

 Hey Teacher . . .

The more creative you are; the more creative I become!

YOURSELF

 Hey Teacher . . .

I am so sorry that you have to wear so many different hats some of which are not yours to wear. I would like to say you wear them all well, thank you!

 # Hey Teacher . . .

When I tell you that
I love you
I mean it!

 Hey Teacher . . .

It's ok if you don't have all the answers
seek advice, help, and counseling from
others.
Really it's OK!

 Hey Teacher . . .

If you are having a bad day take five!

 Hey Teacher . . .

Please deal with your excess baggage because when you don't you bring it to work and store it there and it weighs down the classroom environment and your coworkers.

 # Hey Teacher . . .

Strive for excellence in all that you do.

 Hey Teacher . . .

You are a leader
so please LEAD!

 # Hey Teacher . . .

Life is short so live it to the fullest!

 Hey Teacher . . .

Live today as if it was your last day to live!

 Hey Teacher . . .

Be secure in who you were created to be, don't allow others to validate who you are.

 Hey Teacher . . .

When you feel good about yourself it helps me to feel good about myself.

 Hey Teacher . . .

When you feel good about yourself it shows.
When you feel bad about yourself it shows.

 Hey Teacher . . .

Learn to love yourself because you are fearfully and wonderfully made from the inside out!

 Hey Teacher . . .

May you find pleasure and joy in your job as a teacher because when you do, it impacts the classroom environment; it impacts each individual child's classroom experience and life experience in a positive and healthy way.

 Hey Teacher . . .

When you dislike your job or are burned out from the job it shows, no matter how hard you try to hide it. I know it, I see it, I feel it and am the recipient of it.

 Hey Teacher . . .

Please take care of yourself.

Hey Teacher . . .

Take time for yourself and enjoy life . . . take time to stop and smell the flowers, watch the ants busy at work, lay in the grass and name the shapes of the clouds, count the stars, read a good book, take a hot bubble bath, make yourself a candle light dinner and the list goes on . . .

 # Hey Teacher . . .

Feed your Spirit Man with spiritual food. It's the spiritual food that will help to transform the mind which will transform your life.

 Hey Teacher . . .

Laughter is soooo good for the soul!
So laugh!

SMALL THINGS

 Hey Teacher . . .

Focus on what matters most and the small stuff will work itself out.

Hey Teacher . . .

Even baby steps are steps forward!

 Hey Teacher . . .

Choose your battles wisely; some battles are not yours to fight!

THANK YOUS

 Hey Teacher . . .

Thank you so much for going the extra mile just for me, to make my life a little bit easier!

 # Hey Teacher . . .

You didn't have to do it; but you did and I say thank you!

Hey Teacher . . .

Thank you for helping me to believe in myself!

 Hey Teacher . . .

Thank you for loving me for who I am!

 Hey Teacher . . .

Thank you for being my friend!

 # Hey Teacher . . .

Thank you for helping me to believe I can succeed as long as I try!

 Hey Teacher . . .

Thank you for helping me to see that there are consequences for the decisions I make in life.

 # Hey Teacher . . .

Thank you for respecting me!

 Hey Teacher . . .

If you believe in prayer please pray for me, Lord knows I need it!

Hey Teacher . . .

Hey Teacher . . .

Hey Teacher . . .

Hey Teacher . . .

Hey Teacher . . .

Hey Teacher . . .

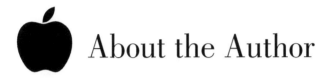# About the Author

Ina Perkins a native of Waterloo, IA now living in Bloomington, IL with her husband Eddie. They have four children and five grandchildren. Ina has a degree in Early Childhood Development and many years of experience working with children and families from all walks of life. She has served children, youth and families in many capacities including but not limited to Assistant Teacher; Preschool Teacher; Summer School Age Program Coordinator; Child Care Center Director; Child Care Center Owner; Head Start Program Manager; and Family Resource Advisor.

Ina has been the instrument that God has used to make a positive impact on the lives of many children and families. Ina has also walked in the shoes of many of the families that God has brought into her life. Ina's heart's desire is to see children living as children and teachers enjoying teaching.